MISHI AND MASHI GO TO BULGARIA

Mishi and Mashi Visit Europe Series

By Mary George

Illustrator Lisa Sacchi

MISHI AND MASHI GO TO BULGARIA by MARY GEORGE
Published by MNG Publishing

www.mishiandmashi.com

Text & illustration copyright © 2022 by Mary George
Illustrations by Lisa Sacchi
Edited by Lor Bingham
Design by Alucia Suceng

First edition

To my daughters

Nicole and Anna-Maria

It's the end of summer and Mishi and Mashi's
family are going on a trip around Bulgaria.
They plan to visit the warm sea and also
enjoy the cool mountains.

They land in the City of Burgas,
which is on the Black Sea.
Heading straight to the Sea Garden, the family
enjoy the beautiful views and the colourful
flower gardens.

The next day, they hire a car and drive to the old coastal town of Nessebar, which is on an island with a big windmill at the entrance.

"This looks like a fairy tale place, Mummy!"
Mashi notes as they stroll around the narrow-paved
streets with lots of little shops around.

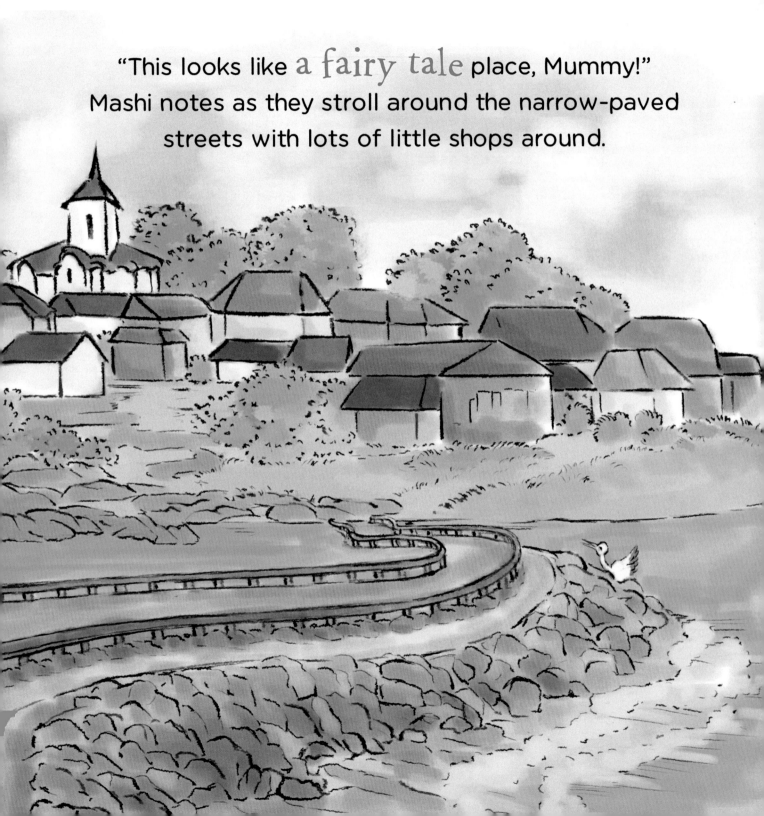

Mishi and Mashi want to stay longer at the sea,
but their parents want to explore the
mysterious Veliko Tarnovo.

"Daddy, who built these houses on the edge
of the mountain?" Mishi asks.
"I guess it was some crazy engineer, like me."
Daddy laughs. "This is the old capital of Bulgaria."
"Where is the new one?" Mashi asks.
"We'll visit soon, and it won't surprise you that
it is near a big mountain too!" Daddy replies.

In the evening, they climb up one of the hills
and enjoy the Sound and Light
Show at the Tsarevets Fortress.
It is a magnificent show of light and music
that follows the history of Bulgaria.

The next day, the family visit the
Rose Valley. "Mummy, why does it smell
so nice here?" the girls ask.

"This town, Kazanlak, is the Capital of Roses
in Bulgaria. They are used in perfumes
and smell beautiful," Mummy replies.
"So we're visiting another capital,
but not the real one? I am getting curious now."
"Don't worry, Mashi. When we get to
Sofia - the capital - it will be worth the wait,"
Mummy explains.

"Are the roses edible, Mummy?
I'm hungry now." Mishi is distracted.

"No, Mishi, they're not edible.
But let's explore the local cuisine!"

They find a little restaurant that serves fresh trout,
caught in the nearby mountain river, and the traditional
Shopska salad with delicious cheese.

"In Bulgaria, we eat cheese with everything,"
a boy calls from a nearby table.
"Even with French fries and melon."

"We love cheese! Where can we go next?"
they ask the local boy, whose name is Ivan.
"Do you want to see a real UFO?"
Mishi and Mashi's eyes widen in surprise.

Of course, the boy was joking. He was referring to a strange-looking round building on top of a mountain, just above his hometown, called Buzludzha.
"It's that what I was talking about," the boy says.

"Come, let's try my favourite treat - buffalo yogurt with wild berries or rose jam!" Ivan calls them. They sit on the grass and enjoy the wonderful views of the UFO-looking building and the wind farm nearby.

The next day, they are on their way to Plovdiv,
but all the signs are in some strange-looking,
neat letters that they can't read.

"Oh no." Daddy is confused.
"The road signs don't make any sense!"

The family are lost! They call Ivan to ask for directions.
"You got lost because the signs are in our
Cyrillic alphabet." He gives them
directions to Plovdiv and says goodbye.

Plovdiv welcomes the family with sunshine and warm weather. They explore the old theatre and watch a short play, as it is still in use. Then they stroll on the little paved roads of the old city.

"I didn't know Plovdiv is a hundred million years old..."
Mashi sighs a little disappointed.
"It also has a fancy, vibrant quarter, let's go there,"
Daddy suggests.

Daddy is talking about the art quarter of
Plovdiv - Kapana. It is filled with colourful little
shops on every corner and many interesting crafts,
museums and galleries.

"You could say Plovdiv is the art capital
of Bulgaria, I suppose," Daddy says.
"Not another capital, Daddy. Sofia is the capital
city and we want to go there!" Mashi insists.

The girls begin to enjoy the local vibe and try as
many new things as they can. Mishi tries doll-making
and Mashi creates some pottery in the local shops.

In their final days, Mishi and Mashi's family
visit Sofia, the capital of Bulgaria.
"We finally made it to the real capital!" Mashi exclaims.

Mummy and Daddy are eager
to see and explore the
glorious Alexander
Nevski Church.
But Mishi and Mashi
find the statue of
St. Sofia much
more fascinating.

"She is the guardian of the city.
As beautiful as her name," Mummy notes.

On the next day, a surprise awaits the girls.
"We're going to a park today," Mummy announces.
"A park in Sofia that is over 2,000
metres high," Daddy adds with a wink.
"It's called Vitosha Park!"

They hop on a cable car that takes them up a
mountain and into a deep forest. Mishi is a little
bit scared of heights, but is distracted by
the beautiful views over the city.

On the top they meet Sylvia, a local ski teacher,
who tells them they must visit again in the winter for
night skiing with a city-view.

"You are right, Sofia was worth
the wait!" the girls agree.

Their final destination
is recommended
by Sylvia - the
Rila Monestary.
"I'll show you around,"
she says kindly.
"This place has a special
feel about it.
You just want to come
back over and over
again, it's the true spirit
of Bulgaria."
"We'd love to visit
again soon!" Mummy
declares.

Mishi and Mashi hug Sylvia goodbye.
She gives them little wooden bottles with
rose water as a gift and... some cheese
for the journey, of course!
"Goodbye, Bulgaria! You have been lovely
and warm. We will see you again!"

MAP of the PLACES MiSHi AND MASHi visited in BULGARIA

Did you find the hidden animal on each page?

The Stork!

Well done!

Now, let's learn some facts about it:

- A carnivore, the White Stork eats a wide range of animal prey, including insects, fish, amphibians, reptiles, small mammals and small birds.

- The White Stork is a long-distance migrant, spending winters in Africa or on the Indian subcontinent. When migrating, it avoids crossing the Mediterranean Sea, because of its cold winds.

- On their return to nest in Europe, the stork families usually find their own nest or a nearby one. The young have to build or find a new one, also usually close to the place where they have been born.

- In Bulgaria, there is a custom to wear a red and white bracelet at the beginning of March and people wear it until they see a stork. It is the symbol of the coming spring. Therefore, the bird is greatly loved and appreciated.

- The village of Belozem has one of the biggest populations of storks in the country. More than 22 stork families live on the school rooftop! There is a national festival of the stork every May and the town has been chosen for European Village of the White Stork.

Source: https://belozemstork.eu and www.birdsinbulgaria.org

Do you want to learn more facts about countries in Europe

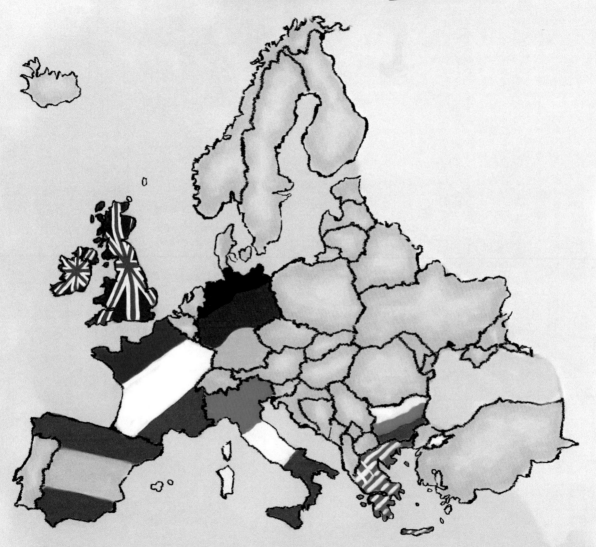

find hidden animals and learn more about them?

Follow our series!
Mishi and Mashi Visit Europe